GW01376985

FIRST ARTS & CRAFTS

Toys and Games

Helen and Peter McNiven
for Sophie, Harry and Jack

With photographs by Chris Fairclough

Wayland

FIRST ARTS & CRAFTS

This series of books aims to introduce children to as wide a range of media approaches, techniques and equipment as possible, and to extend these experiences into ideas for further development. The National Curriculum proposals for art at Key Stage One place particular emphasis on the appreciation of art in a variety of styles from different cultures and times throughout history. The series broadly covers the National Curriculum attainment targets 1) Investigating and Making and 2) Knowledge and Understanding, but recognizes that circumstances and facilities can vary hugely. Children should experiment with, and add to, all the ideas in these books, working from imagination and observation. They should also work with others, where possible, in groups and as a class. You will find suggestions for and comments about particular sections of work in the Notes for parents/teachers at the end of the book. They are by no means prescriptive and can be added to and adapted. Unless a particular type of paint or glue is specified, any type can be used. Aprons and old newspapers provide protection for clothes and surfaces when working with papier mâché, glue, paints, etc. Above all, the most important thing is that children enjoy art in every sense of the word. Have fun!

Titles in this series

Collage, Drawing, Masks, Models, Painting, Printing, Puppets, Toys and Games

First published in 1994
by Wayland (Publishers) Ltd, 61 Western Road, Hove
East Sussex BN3 1JD, England
© Copyright 1994 Wayland (Publishers) Ltd
Series planned and produced by The Square Book Company

British Library Cataloguing in Publication Data
McNiven, Helen
Toys and Games. - (First Arts & Crafts Series)
I. Title II. McNiven, Peter III. Fairclough, Chris IV. Series
745.592
ISBN 0 7502 1014 1

Photographs by Chris Fairclough
Designed by Howland ■ Northover
Edited by Joanna Bentley
Printed and bound in Italy by G. Canale & C.S.p.A., Turin

Contents

Toys and games	4
Giant snap	6
Jigsaws	8
Jumping Jack doll	10
Flying high	12
Fishing game	14
Jolly jumpers	16
Crazy golf	18
Calico cat	20
Four seasons game	22
Hoopla - ball in the hole	24
Trojan horse	26
Noah's Ark	28
Notes for parents/teachers	30
Further information	32
Glossary	
Index	

Toys and games

Everybody likes toys and in museums you will see toys from earliest times. In this picture you can see a selection of old toys and games.

Many games, particularly games played outside, are very old indeed.

Toys and games can help us to learn things like balancing, throwing and memory skills. But most of all, toys are fun.

4

Try to visit a museum and see old toys. How have they changed? Do you still play the same games?

Many modern toys are made of plastics, although you can still buy wooden hand-made toys. These toys will last a lifetime. Your grandparents may still have their old dolls' house or rocking horse.

In this book you will see how to make your own toys and games with very simple materials. Not only will you have many happy hours with your toy or game, but you will have made it too.

Giant snap

Look at this picture of everyday objects. How many are the same? Snap is a game where you win two cards if they are both the same. You can play this with a pack of cards you have made yourself.

You will need:
Card or 20 plain postcards
Scissors
Ruler
Pencil
Paints or felt-tipped pens

To make your cards:

- Cut out twenty rectangles measuring 15cm x 10cm from a large sheet of card, or use twenty plain postcards.
- Draw a simple object from your home, like a cup or a spoon. Either trace it or draw it again, exactly the same, on another rectangle of card. Colour them brightly.

- Now draw nine other objects twice and colour them.
- Colour the backs of the cards all the same. You could use coloured wavy lines or stick on coloured or patterned paper.

To play snap with a friend, mix up all the cards you have made. Give your friend ten and yourself ten. Make sure the cards are facing down. Take it in turns to turn your cards face up. When the pictures on two cards match, the first person to shout 'Snap!' wins them both.

7

Jigsaws

Park near Lu 1938 by Paul Klee (1879-1940).

You will need:
Thin card
Paints and felt-tipped pens
Pencil
Ruler
Scissors

Look at these two pictures. One uses circles and swirling shapes and the other uses squares and rectangles.

- Draw or paint a colourful picture using round and swirly shapes.
- Draw or paint another picture with lines and rectangular shapes. You can copy these pictures if you like.

- With a black pen draw straight lines down and across your swirly picture.
- Draw wavy lines across your second picture.
- Cut along the black lines and you have made two jigsaws. Don't get them muddled up!

Which is easier to put back together? Test your friends and see how well they can put them together.

Jumping Jack doll

This picture of bathers having fun at the seaside was painted more than 70 years ago. Look at the old-fashioned swimsuits. You're going to make a bather into a moving picture!

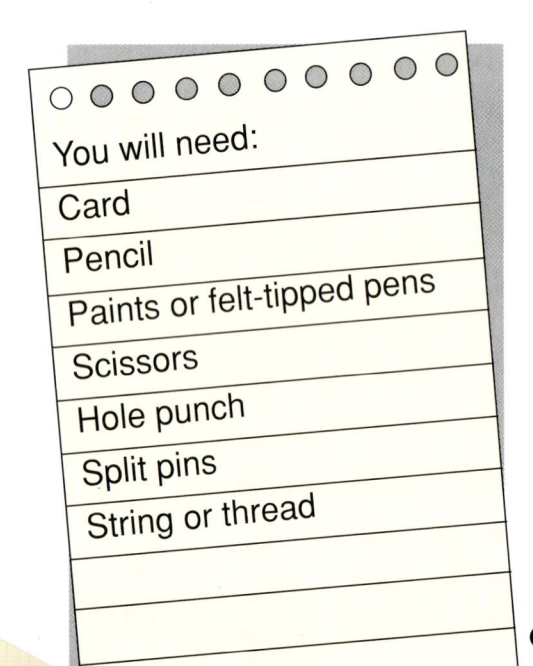

You will need:
- Card
- Pencil
- Paints or felt-tipped pens
- Scissors
- Hole punch
- Split pins
- String or thread

Bathers, Biarritz, Summer 1918 by Pablo Picasso (1881-1973).

- Draw a man's or lady's body on a piece of card. You could copy one of the bathers from this painting.
- Draw arms and legs separately.
- Carefully cut out the body and the arms and legs.
- Colour in a brightly painted swimsuit.

- Punch holes in the tops of the arms and legs, where they will join the body.
- Fix them on loosely by pushing split pins through the body and the arm or leg.
- Now string the arms and legs to a central string as shown.

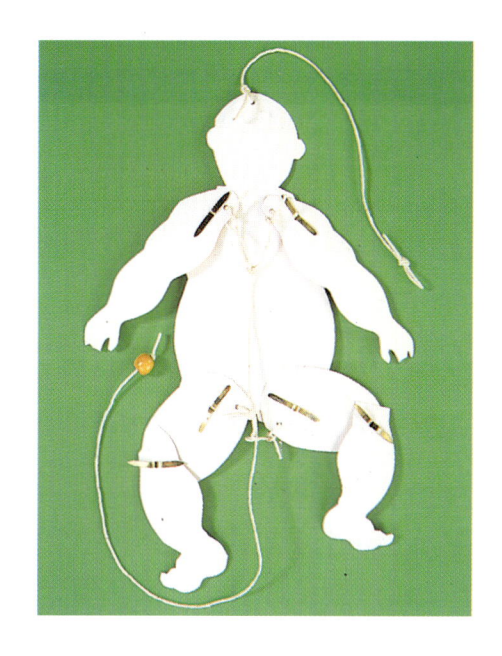

Pull the string and watch your bather jump. Why not make a whole family? Your family perhaps!

Flying high

The kite has been around for 2,500 years. The biggest one ever made was flown by 150 people. The Chinese and Japanese have always loved kites. You can make your own pocket kite which will fly quite well in a light wind.

You will need:
- Paper
- Ruler
- Pencil
- Stapler or glue
- Tissue paper
- Hole punch
- Paints
- Garden stick
- Thread

- Take a piece of paper 20cm x 28cm and fold it in half – you will now have a piece 20cm x 14cm.
- Mark 1cm in from the fold at the top, and 1cm in from the open edge at the bottom.
- Draw a diagonal line between these marks and fold one half of the paper along it. In the same way, draw a line and fold the other half of the paper – these are your wings.

12

- Glue or staple the paper together along the first fold. Add a tissue tail. Punch three small holes, 1cm apart, starting 4cm down from the top. This is your keel, and you put the thread through one of the holes – which hole you use depends on the strength of the wind.
- Decorate your kite brightly. Tape a piece of garden stick across the kite from corner to corner. Attach a length of thread and you're off.

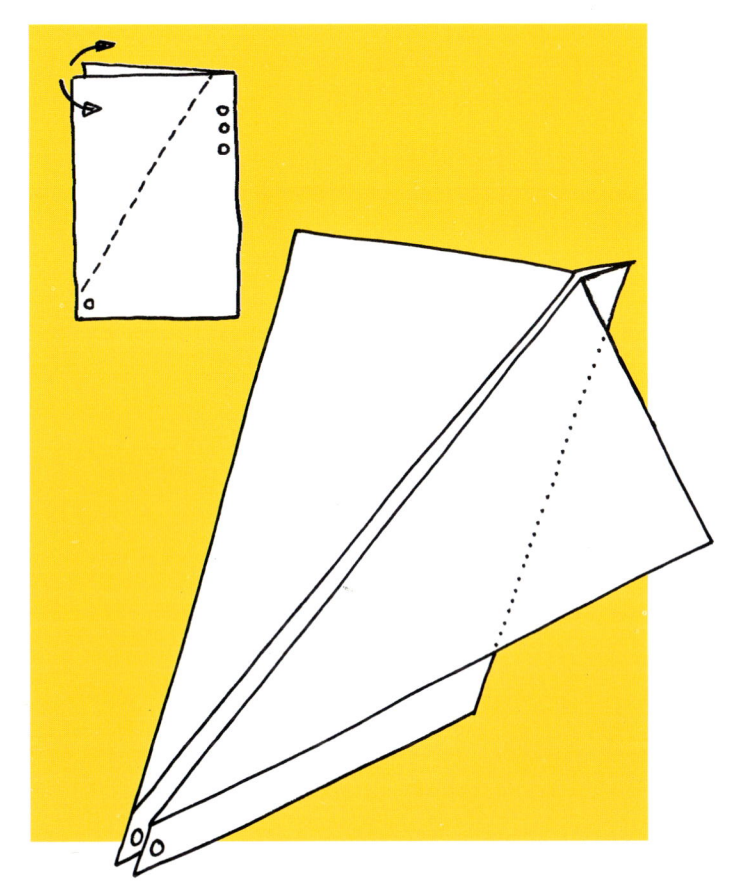

Fishing game

There is a whole world of lovely creatures living under the sea. Many of them have strange shapes, patterns and strong colours.

You can make your own creatures and catch them.

You will need:
- Plastic milk cartons
- Waterproof felt-tipped pens
- Scissors
- Corks
- Wire
- Plasticine
- Knife
- Garden stick
- String
- A bowl or tank of water

- Draw all sorts of underwater creatures on to some plastic from a milk carton.
- Cut them out and decorate them brightly with waterproof felt tips.
- Ask an adult to cut a slit along a cork. Slide your creature on to the cork.
- Make a small loop out of wire and push it into the other side of the cork. Add a small Plasticine weight to the bottom of each creature.

- Push the other creatures you have made on to corks too.
- Now make a fishing rod. Tie some string on to one end of a garden stick. Tie a curved piece of wire on to the end of the string.
- Put all your creatures into a bowl or tank of water and see how many you can catch. Challenge a friend to a fishing match.

15

Jolly jumpers

This is a game about a race between a tortoise and a hare. It comes from a story by Aesop. Who do you think will win?

You will need:
- Card
- Pencil
- Scissors
- Ruler
- Paints or felt-tipped pens

The hare and the tortoise 1912 from Aesop's Fables by Arthur Rackham.

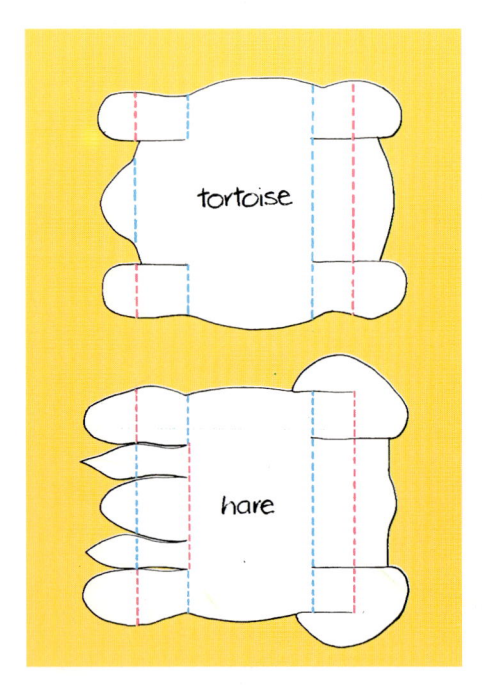

- Take a piece of card 30cm x 21cm and draw outlines on it as shown.
- Make a tortoise jumper first, by cutting along all the black lines.

16

- Fold blue lines down and red lines up – you now have a head, four legs and a tail.
- Colour your jumper to make it look more like a tortoise.
- Make the hare jumper the same way but shaped and coloured to look like a hare.
- Put your finger at the back of your jumper's body and press down. Let go and watch it jump.

You can make a track and race with your friends. Or you can see who can make their jumper leap the farthest.

Crazy golf

Lots of people's favourite game is golf, in which you have to get a small ball down a hole by hitting it a long way with sticks called clubs. In this game you must try <u>not</u> to get the ball down the hole!

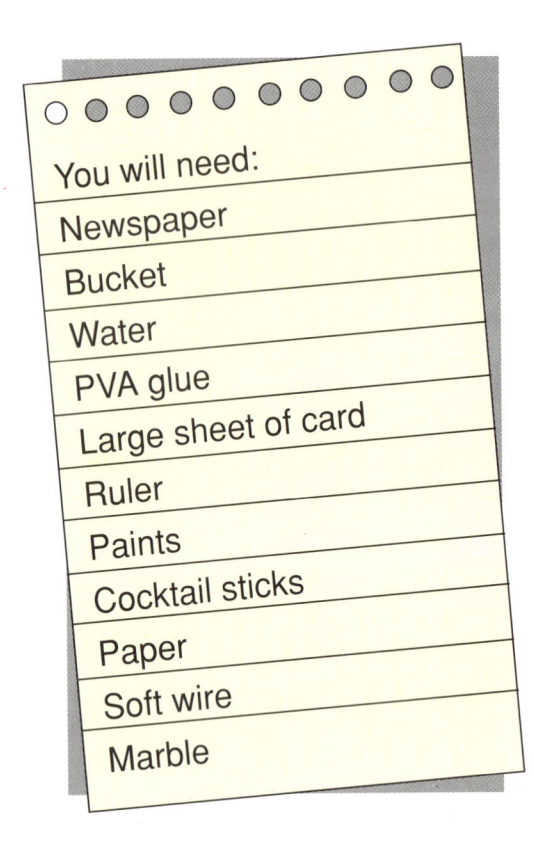

You will need:
- Newspaper
- Bucket
- Water
- PVA glue
- Large sheet of card
- Ruler
- Paints
- Cocktail sticks
- Paper
- Soft wire
- Marble

First, make some papier mâché pulp. Ask an adult to help you.

- Tear lots of old newspaper into small bits. Put the pieces into a bucket and cover them with warm water.
- Leave the bucket like this overnight. Then, carefully pour the water out, leaving the wet newspaper behind.
- Using your hands, mix enough PVA glue into the newspaper to make it soft and sticky.

- Take a large piece of card and cover it with a layer of papier mâché pulp about 1cm high.
- With your finger press in a wiggly groove all over the card.
- Make holes to the side of the path every so often. At the end of your path make a little hollow. Make coloured paper flags, stick them on to cocktail sticks and push them in around the paths. Push in wire hoops too.
- Leave the papier mâché to dry and then paint it.

Now, by rocking the toy, see if you can get a marble round the golf course without it going down the holes.

Calico cat

This is a sculpture by American artist Claes Oldenburg. He is famous for making sculptures of everyday objects out of soft materials.

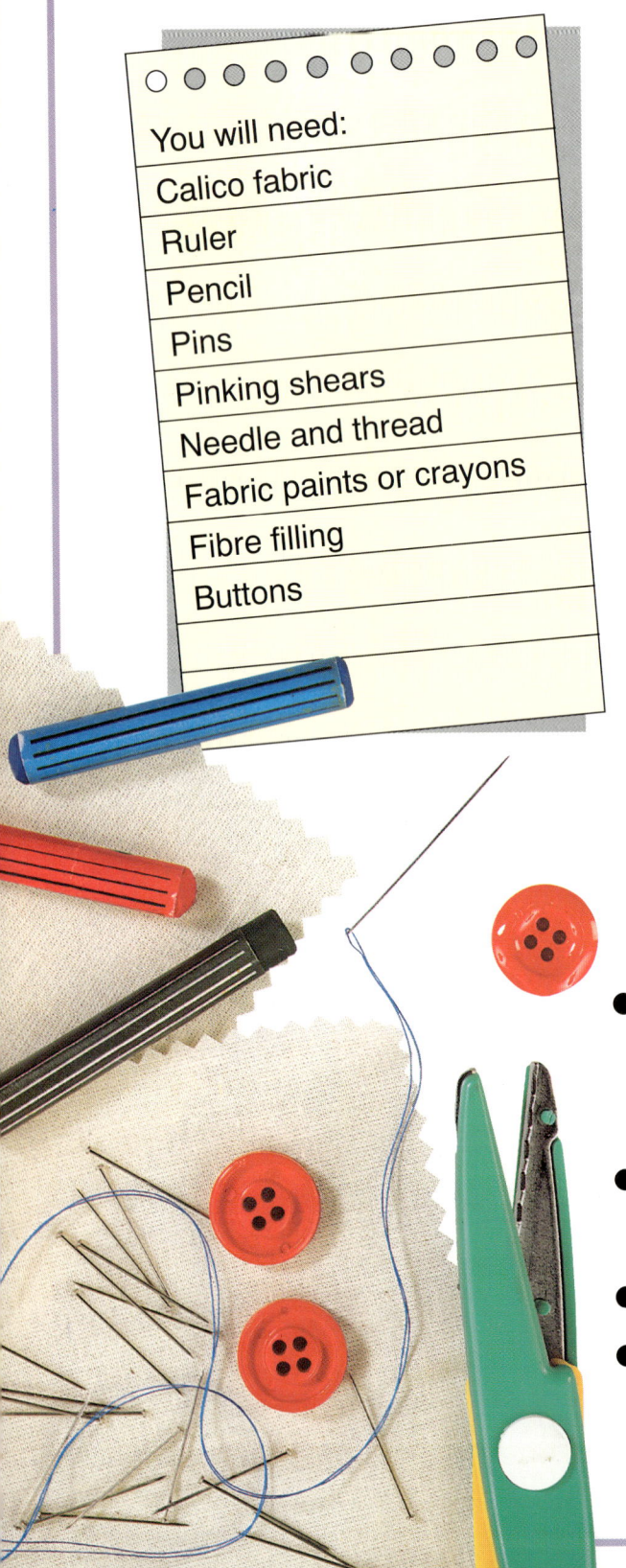

You will need:
- Calico fabric
- Ruler
- Pencil
- Pins
- Pinking shears
- Needle and thread
- Fabric paints or crayons
- Fibre filling
- Buttons

Giant Hamburger 1962 by Claes Oldenburg (born 1929).

You can make a soft toy cat, a rag doll, a car, or anything you like.

- Take a piece of calico fabric that measures 40cm x 30cm and fold it in half to 20cm x 30cm
- Draw a large cat or car in pencil on the calico.
- Pin around the inside of your drawing.
- Cut out your shape with pinking shears, following the line.

- Take the pins out. Now you have two pieces: the front and the back of your toy. Paint and decorate them with fabric paints or crayons. Remember to paint the front of one piece and the back of the other.
- Put your pieces together with the painted sides facing out. Sew them together with a needle and thread, using small running stitches 1cm in from the edge. Leave a 6cm opening for the stuffing.
- Stuff your toy carefully and firmly with fibre filling until it is plump.
- Sew up the opening. Sew on buttons for decoration, like eyes or car wheels.

21

Four seasons game

This is a game to make and then play with friends. Two or four people can play it.

You will need:
Card
Ruler
Pencil
Paints or felt tips
Scissors
Cocktail stick

Spring

Summer

Autumn

Winter

First you must make your four playing boards. One will be spring, one summer, one autumn and one winter.

- Divide four pieces of card measuring 21cm x 14cm into two rows of three squares. This gives you six 7cm squares on each card.
- Now think of ... things to show each season. What about a blue boat for summer ... and a green plant for spring? Draw one in each box on your card. Colour each picture in a different colour. Use red, yellow, blue, purple, orange and green. You will have six pictures for one season on each card.
- Now, with more card, make 24 cards measuring 5cm x 5cm. Paint four of each colour and draw the same seasons pictures on them.
- To make a simple dice, cut out a hexagon of card and mark it into six equal sections. Colour each section one of the six colours. Push a cocktail stick though the centre.

Give each player one seasons board. When you spin your dice, the colour it falls to is the colour card you pick up. Place the card over the picture on your board of the same colour. The first person to cover their seasons board wins.

23

Hoopla - ball in the hole

The fair is great fun, but it costs money. This game is free, and fun to make too.

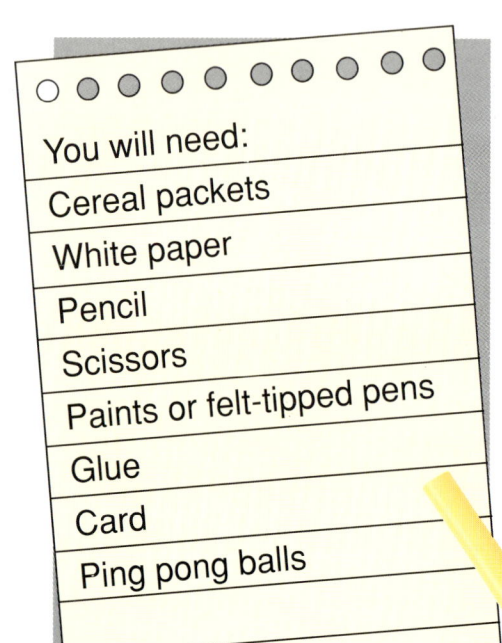

You will need:
- Cereal packets
- White paper
- Pencil
- Scissors
- Paints or felt-tipped pens
- Glue
- Card
- Ping pong balls

- Take three or more cereal packets. Cover the front of each with paper or white paint.
- Draw on some big faces with mouths of different sizes.

- Cut out the mouths so that they are holes in the packets.
- Paint the faces brightly.
- Stick your boxes together in a line.
- Stand 2 metres from them and see if you can throw ping pong balls into the mouths. You will score more for getting the ball into a smaller mouth.
- Stick pointed hats or cardboard flowers on and try to throw small card hoops on to them.

Trojan horse

An old Greek story tells us how a giant wooden horse on wheels was used to trick the people of Troy during the Trojan War. The horse was a gift from their enemies, the Greeks. The horse was taken into the city, but that night, Greek soldiers hiding inside the horse, climbed down out of a secret door.

Perhaps this was the first horse on wheels. You can make one too.

You will need:
- Cardboard box
- Cardboard tubes
- Gummed tape
- Card
- Newspaper
- Wallpaper paste
- Cereal packet
- Paints
- Drinking straw
- 2 garden sticks

Trojan horse.

Look at pictures of horses or toy horses – or better still a real horse.

- Take a cardboard box for a body and roll up some card to make legs. Use tubes for the neck and head and card for the mane and tail. Stick these on to the body with gummed tape.

- Now cover your model with torn newspaper and wallpaper paste. Glue your finished horse on to a cereal packet.
- Leave it to dry, then paint it.
- Make wheels from card. Push two garden sticks through the packet and slide the wheels on to the ends. Use pieces of straw as washers between the box and the wheel.

27

Noah's Ark

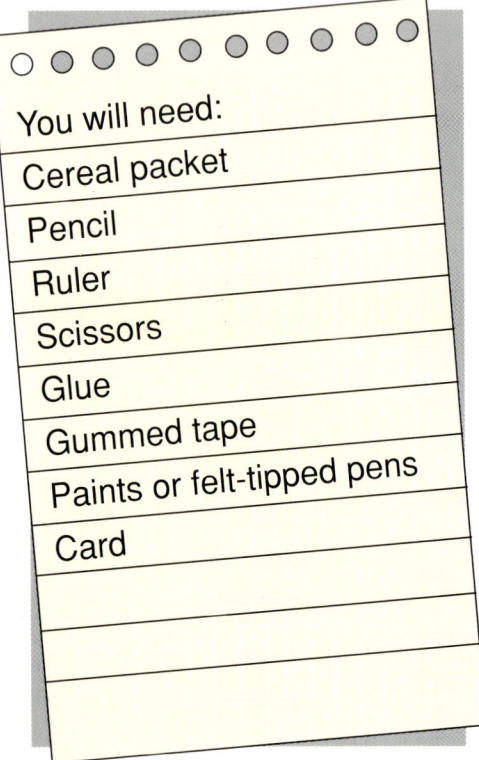

You will need:
- Cereal packet
- Pencil
- Ruler
- Scissors
- Glue
- Gummed tape
- Paints or felt-tipped pens
- Card

One of the most beautiful old toys is a Noah's Ark. They used to be made of wood and often had over 100 pairs of hand-carved wooden animals.

- All you need is a cereal packet to make your own Noah's Ark.
- Follow the simple step-by-step diagrams for marking out, cutting and folding your ark.
- To put it together, turn your pieces inside out so that the packet markings are on the inside.

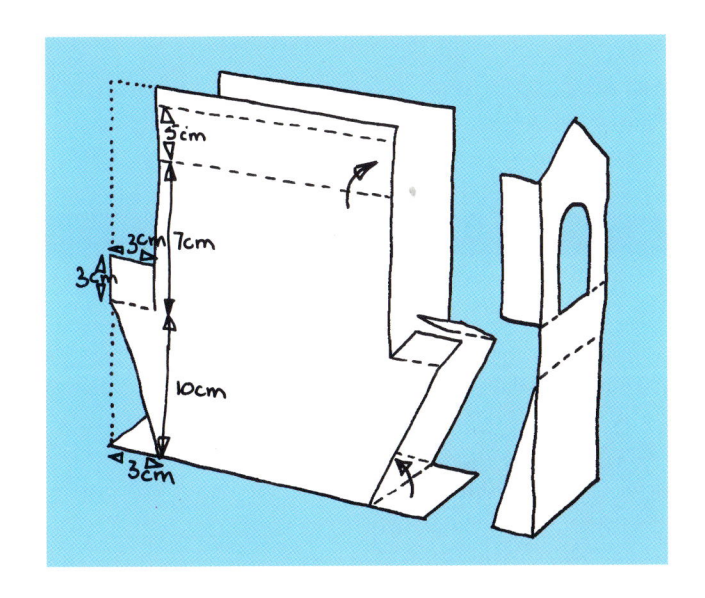

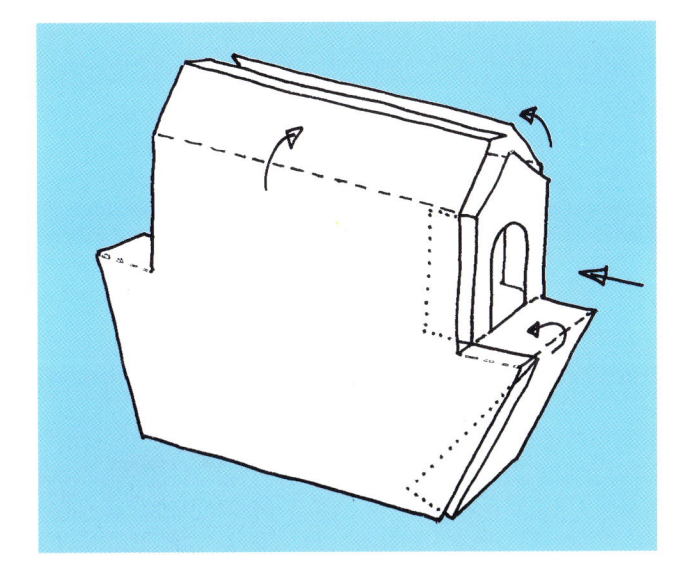

- Glue the 'ship' together first at the base and then the roof.
- Next, glue in the sides of the house and then tape all the corners with gummed tape.
- Colour your ark brightly with paints or felt tips.
- Make pairs of paper or card animals to fill your ark. Don't forget Noah and his wife.

Notes for parents/teachers

FIRST ARTS & CRAFTS: TOYS AND GAMES shows that toys and games are fun, and that there is no reason why they should not be a learning process as well. The toys and games in this book have been chosen to develop small children's memory and and motor skills, while also introducing them to a wider world of experiences. Simple mathematical and scientific ideas are introduced, and many of the projects will form the basis of thematic discussion. As in all the books in the series many of the projects relate to the fine arts and all are specifically designed to increase visual awareness.

Giant snap 6-7
Encourage children to look around them – they will be surprised how often things are duplicated. They should work from source if possible, drawing things in front of them, and observing colours and patterns. The home is a good theme, but simple animal, bird or plant forms, like flowers, leaves, etc, would work well visually and would also be instructive. They can practise re-copying their images, or trace them by drawing over the outline on to tracing paper and then redrawing firmly over this on to another piece of card – the graphite is transferred by pressure. They can also use the cards for a matching memory game.

Jigsaws 8-9
Many works of art can be used, or children can make up their own 'abstractions'. Pictures with bold shapes and colours work well and are simpler than traditional fine art jigsaws. Graph paper is a great help for geometric work, and for circular, swirling images they can draw round a variety of circular objects of different sizes. Artists to look at include Matisse, van Gogh, Mondrian, Kandinsky, Klee, Ben Nicholson and Patrick Heron. This project can lead to discussion about colour, pattern and balance of coloured spaces. 'Wavy scissors' or pinking shears can be used for cutting.

Jumping Jack doll 10-11
The seaside postcard is just one idea – children may have pictures of themselves at the sea or doing other things that they would like to 'animate'. Pictures from magazines can be stuck to card and made to move, or they too can be copied. Sport and dance, or animals, would make good themes and a U shape of card could be used to attach a figure to a relevant background. It can be attached above the mechanism or provision made for the thread to run, unhindered, through it. This project explains simple principles of mechanics.

Flying high 12-13
The kite responds well in a light breeze. Bigger kites can be made to the same proportions. The fixing of the line is relative to wind strength and balance – trial and error is the only way to solve it. This project is a good introduction to the concept of flight, drag, lift, etc.

Fishing game 14-15
Encourage children to look at a variety of underwater life, either by visiting an aquarium, the seaside or using books. Discuss why they are coloured like they are (camouflage, warning, etc.). The children can invent their own creatures, like mermaids, if they wish (catching a mermaid could be a minus point in a game). Swirl the water to make the game more difficult. Use a stop watch too. By adjusting the wire loop to left or right a good sense of balance can be obtained. Hand-eye co-ordination is learnt here.

Jolly jumpers 16-17
Jumping dogs, cats, frogs or horses can be made to almost any scale as long as the card has a good bit of 'spring' in it – this of course can lead on to discussion about springs, energy and propulsion.

Crazy golf 18-19
The course can be set into a box if you wish, with a ramp back up to the start. A maze using strips of card can also be made. Each require dexterity to get from one end to the other.

Calico cat 20-21
There are a variety of paints and pens on the market for this purpose, or you could combine printmaking techniques. Pinking shears are needed to prevent fraying. Cut up old nylon tights will make an adequate filling. Any soft toy can be made (dolls, animals, houses, etc.) and a variety of decorations can be added. A group project could be a farm or a street.

Four seasons game 22-23
This project does many things – it teaches an awareness of the seasons, and associations we have with them, although other themes could be used. It teaches colour theory, primary and secondary, and the basic geometric formula of a radius fitting six times to the circumference of a circle – amazing really! The sizes given relate to the size of a standard sheet of thin A4 card.

Hoopla - ball in the hole 24-25
There is no limit to the number of packets used, and other shapes can be used too. Slim, pointed hats can be added and used for hoopla with card quoits. Decoration can be enhanced by adding texture like wool for hair, egg box bits for nose, etc. This is a good game for hand-eye co-ordination and for adding up scores.

Trojan horse 26-27
The size is up to you and this could be a group activity. A secret opening can easily be cut in underneath the belly. Encourage children to think about form as they model. Any sculpture project involves seeing in the round. This is an excellent project to introduce children to myth and legend. You could put any other animal on wheels too.

Noah's Ark 28-29
This is simplicity itself to make and can be textured with planks, roof tiles, shutters, etc. You could also add on a more prominent bow and perhaps a matchbox house on the stern. Remind the children that not all male and female animals look the same. A pairing game could be made up. The measurements are for a 750g packet, but you may wish to work larger. Turning the card inside out makes it take paint much more easily.

Further information

Glossary

Aesop A Greek author who wrote stories about animals thousands of years ago.
Calico A plain, unbleached cotton fabric.
Dice A six-sided shape, usually a square block, with a different number on each face.
Hexagon A six-sided shape with sides of equal size.
Keel The lowest part of a ship or kite that helps to keep it well-balanced and steady.
Noah's ark According to the Bible, the ship in which Noah, his family and a pair of each kind of animal were saved from a great flood.

Pinking shears Scissors that cut with a zig-zag edge.
PVA glue A water based glue.
Running stitch A simple sewing stitch – the needle and thread are passed in and out of the fabric in a straight line.
Split pins Pins with two ends. When the pin is pushed through something, the two ends are bent backwards to hold the pin in place.
Washers In this book, small pieces of plastic that are used to prevent wheels from rubbing.
Texture The feel or look of a surface.

Index

animals 16-17, 20-21, 26-27, 28-29
card games 6-7, 22-23
    four seasons game 22-23
    snap 6-7
dolls 10-11, 20-21
fish 14-15
golf 18-19

horses 26-27
jigsaws 8-9
kites 12-13
Noah's Ark 28-29
papier mâché 18-19
sewing 20-21
soft toys 20-21

Acknowledgements

The publishers wish to thank the following for the use of photographs:
Abstract p.8 by Bridget Howland.
Park near Lu 1938 p.8 by Paul Klee, by kind permission of Paul-Klee-Stiftung Kunstmuseum, Bern © DACS 1994.
Visual Arts Library for *Bathers* 1918 p.10 by Pablo Picasso © DACS 1994.
Giant Hamburger 1962 p.20 by Claes Oldenburg, reproduced by kind permission of Oldenburg/van Bruggen and The Art Gallery of Ontario, Toronto.
Robert Harding Picture Library Ltd for *Kite Festival, California* p.12 by Jon Gardey, and for *Trojan Horse, Troy, Turkey* p.26 by Michael Short.
Mary Evans Picture Library for *The hare and the tortoise* (Aesop) 1912 p.16 by Arthur Rackham.
Popperfoto for the picture of the golfer p.18.
Noah's Ark p.28 from the Museum of Childhood, Bethnal Green reproduced by courtesy of the Board of Trustees of the Victoria and Albert Museum.
All other photographs © Chris Fairclough Colour Library.
The publishers also wish to thank our models Kim, Kerry, Manlai, Katie and Jeremy.